GREAT CITIES OF THE WORLD

BAGHDAD

NIKKI VAN DER GAAG AND FELICITY ARBUTHNOT

WORLD ALMANAC® LIBRARY

Please visit our web site at: www.worldalmanaclibrary.com
For a free color catalog describing World Almanac® Library's list of high-quality books
and multimedia programs, call 1-800-848-2928 (USA) or 1-800-387-3178 (Canada).
World Almanac® Library's fax: (414) 332-3567.

Library of Congress Cataloging-in-Publication Data

Gaag, Nikki van der.
    Baghdad / by Nikki van der Gaag and Felicity Arbuthnot.
        p. cm. — (Great cities of the world)
    Includes bibliographical references and index.
    ISBN 0-8368-5049-1 (lib.bdg.)
    ISBN 0-8368-5209-5 (softcover)
    1. Baghdad (Iraq)—Juvenile literature.   I. Arbuthnot, Felicity.   II. Title.   III. Series.
DS79.9.B25G33   2005
956.7'47—dc22   2005043587

First published in 2006 by
World Almanac® Library
A Member of the WRC Media Family of Companies
330 West Olive Street, Suite 100
Milwaukee, WI 53212 USA

Copyright © 2006 by World Almanac® Library.

Produced by Discovery Books
Editors: Valerie Weber and Kathryn Walker
Series designers: Laurie Shock, Keith Williams
Designer and page production: Rob Norridge
Photo researcher: Rachel Tisdale
Diagrams: Rob Norridge
Maps: Stefan Chabluk
World Almanac® Library editorial direction: Mark J. Sachner
World Almanac® Library editor: Gini Holland
World Almanac® Library art direction: Tammy West
World Almanac® Library graphic design: Scott M. Krall
World Almanac® Library production: Jessica Morris

Photo credits: akg-images/Erich Lessing: p. 8; akg-images/VISIOARS: p. 11; Art Directors and Trip/Jane Sweeney:
pp. 4, 10, 15, 18; Corbis/Ed Kashi: cover and title page; Getty Images/AFP/Awad Awad: p. 26; Getty Images/AFP/Sabah
Arar: p. 28; Getty Images/AFP/Ramzi Haidar: p. 16; Getty Images/AFP/Roslan Rahman: p. 29; Getty Images/AFP/
Brendan Sialowski: p. 35; Getty Images/Ahmad Al-Rubaye: p. 20; Getty Images/Marco di Lauro: p. 34; Getty Images/
Hulton Archive: p. 13; Getty Images/Wathiq Kuzaie: p. 21; Getty Images/Spencer Platt: p. 37; Jenny Matthews:
pp. 19, 24, 31, 36, 39, 40; Panos Pictures/Martin Adler: pp. 7, 25; Panos Pictures/Editing/Hie Lam Duc: pp. 23, 32.

Cover: This street scene shows people in Baghdad's Kadhimiya district, walking in front of the Kadhimain Shrine.
The shrine is the third holiest site for Shiite Muslims.

Printed in Canada

1 2 3 4 5 6 7 8 9 09 08 07 06 05

Contents

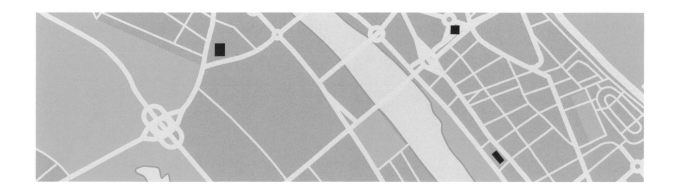

Introduction

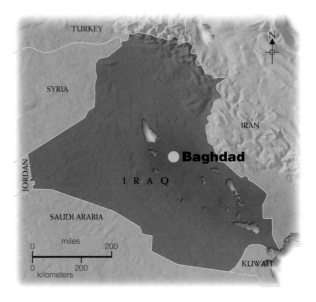

For twenty-three out of the last twenty-five years, Baghdad has been a city at war. Both the city itself and its people bear the scars of this violence, which began in 1980. In 2003, the United States and Great Britain invaded Iraq, and the U.S. Army occupied Baghdad, the capital.

Since then, the city has become an increasingly dangerous place to live. Ordinary people are caught in the battle between the foreign armies and those who

◄ *Wherever you go in Baghdad you see domes and minarets covered with gold leaf or sparkling blue tiles, like the one in this picture. Many belong to shrines or mosques, each with its own story.*

are prepared to use violence to get them to leave. These people are typically described as insurgents, but some people in Iraq see them as resistance fighters. Despite the constant fighting, Baghdad remains a beautiful and historic city with a rich past and a vibrant cultural life.

City of Contradictions

Baghdad is a young city, where 45 percent of the population is under the age of eighteen. It is also an ancient city, located in

the region where civilization began, and the law, the wheel, the first written records, and plow were invented. While Iraq currently contains the world's second-largest reserves of oil, which should make it rich, Baghdad's people go hungry. It is a city at war, where most of the people want peace.

The City between Two Rivers

Baghdad lies between the Tigris and the Euphrates Rivers. Often mentioned in the Bible, the rivers have always provided both water and a means of transportation to and within the city. The Tigris's two principal sources both start in Turkey, but 80 percent of the river runs through Iraq. Along its course, the Tigris passes through some of the country's major cities, such as Mosul, Tikrit, Samarra, and Baghdad. A dam on the Tigris at Samarra improves control of the floods that sometimes happen when snow melts in the mountains between March and May. At Al Qurna, believed to be the site of the Garden of Eden, the Tigris joins with the Euphrates. For the remaining 106 miles (170 kilometers) before it empties into the Persian Gulf, the waterway is known as the Shatt al Arab, where Sinbad the Sailor is supposed to have set off on his travels.

Geography

Surrounded on all sides by desert, Baghdad nestles in the heart of Iraq. To the west is the long road through the desert to the country of Jordan; the way north leads to the mountains of the Kurdish area and then to Turkey. South of Baghdad lies the port of Basra and Iraq's narrow access to the Persian Gulf, which it shares with Kuwait. To the east stretches the border with Iran. Baghdad is the transportation hub of the country, with main roads linking it to the south and west.

"The width of the Tigris in Baghdad is about four hundred yards, a noble stream. It is the only sweet, fresh thoroughfare of the town—not clear water, but lion colored. . . . Its broad, flowing surface is dyed by the same earth of which the houses and minarets on its banks are built, so that all is one, in tawny harmony. Its low winter mists in early morning . . . its many craft evolved through centuries . . . all this a perpetual joy."

—Freya Stark, British writer and photographer who traveled extensively in the Middle East, in *Baghdad Sketches*, 1932.

Baghdad's Layout

Baghdad is an impressive and complex city, with several centers. Many bridges, complete with highways, connect the two sides of the city, which straddles the Tigris River. The eastern part of the city is called Rusafa and the western is Al Karkh. Both these parts are also divided into many districts, each with its own center. The main areas of activity are around Sa'adoun and Al Jamoun Streets, on the east bank of the Tigris.

The streets of Baghdad are wide, and the city feels very spacious. Most buildings were constructed in the 1970s, but there are many beautiful old ones as well. With

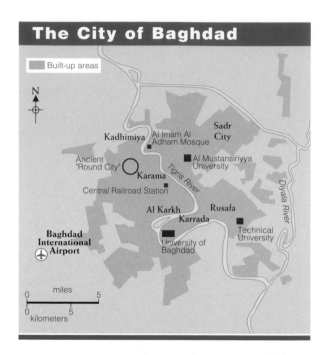

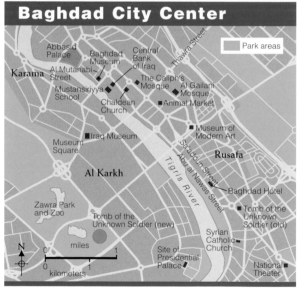

intricately carved arches and ceilings, Abbasid Palace, which was probably built in the late 1100s, is the oldest. The city has many parks, museums, and a zoo; the animals have suffered as well through the years of war and sanctions.

▲ *The Iraqi national kayaking team practices in June 2004 on the Tigris River that flows through the center of war-torn Baghdad. The area is insecure, however, and the team has been shot at during training.*

Climate

Like the rest of Iraq, Baghdad has mild to cool winters; the temperature can fall to 48° Fahrenheit (9° Celsius) in January and February. The summers are dry, hot, and cloudless, and temperatures can climb to more than 104° F (40° C). The average temperature throughout the year is about 73° F (23° C). Little rain falls here, only an average of 1 inch (2.5 centimeters) in the winter months and none in the summer. The total yearly rainfall is about 6 inches (15 cm) a year.

CHAPTER 1

History of Baghdad

It was in Mesopotamia, on the fertile plains of the area now called Iraq, where people first settled down from a hunting and gathering lifestyle and began to farm in about 6500 B.C. A civilization called Sumer arose in about 3500 B.C. The Sumerians built irrigation canals that helped tame the flooding of the Euphrates and Tigris Rivers. They invented a form of writing called cuneiform as well as sailboats and also developed board games. Trade routes to Sumer brought foreign metals in exchange for spices, silks, wines, carpets, and gold.

Over the centuries, the Babylonians, Assyrians, Persians from present-day Iran, and Greeks all ruled the area in turn. In A.D. 637, Arabs from the Arabian Peninsula conquered the Persians, who had again ousted the Greeks. They brought the religion of Islam and its followers of the Prophet Muhammad to Iraq.

Caliph Abu Jaafur al Mansur of the Abbasid dynasty, who were descendants of the Prophet Muhammad's uncle, founded Baghdad in 762. Sleeping at the site of a former Persian village, Al Mansur declared that he had spent "the sweetest, gentlest night on earth" there. He decided to build a

◄ *This statue of a man praying dates back to the Sumerian dynasty, which ruled Iraq for almost a thousand years, from 3500 B.C. to 2340 B.C. The statue belongs to the Iraq Museum in Baghdad.*

The House of Wisdom

During Baghdad's first five centuries, it was probably the most famous place of learning in the world. It drew scholars of various religions from around the world to its Bayt al Hikma (House of Wisdom). At this great library, people studied the humanities and sciences, including mathematics, astronomy, medicine, chemistry, zoology, and geography, as well as alchemy and astrology. They helped preserve the knowledge of ancient civilizations and brought the wisdom of the Arab world, including mathematics and medicine, to Europe. Translators worked on Chinese, Indian, Greek, and Latin books brought from afar.

Many people could read, and paper was widely available. The first paper arrived in Iraq from China, probably along the silk route via Samarkand (which lies in what is now Uzbekistan) during the eighth century, long before it reached Europe. Shortly afterward, a paper mill was established in Baghdad, and by the end of the tenth century, paper had replaced parchment and papyrus in the Arab world.

great city and laid the first brick himself "in the name of God." It was a round city surrounded by thick walls. In the middle of the circle stood the Great Mosque and the caliph's palace, known as the Golden Gate, with its huge green dome. Outside the walls surrounding the palace and mosque lay housing for the army. A ring of civilian houses encircled the army's space and were themselves surrounded by thick walls. The merchants' quarters and marketplace lay outside the walls.

Baghdad would become the most splendid metropolis of its time. A complex irrigation system fed the countryside, so the city had plenty of food, including fruits and vegetables. Between 786 and 800, it became the focus of power, wealth, and learning. Originally called the "Garden of Justice" (*Bagh-dad* in Persian), it became known as the "City of Peace."

Rivers of Blood

Baghdad has historically been a place of wars, however, not peace. The city has survived twenty-one bloody invasions. Each time, it has rebuilt itself, and the people have started their lives over again. In Baghdad, history has a habit of repeating itself.

In 1055, Tughril Beg, a warrior from Turkey, conquered Iraq and founded the mighty Seljuk dynasty, which ruled the area until the Christian Crusaders defeated them. The Crusaders came from Europe in 1096 to fight for what they called the Holy Land, the area where, according to the Bible, Jesus Christ lived and died. They particularly wanted Jerusalem because of its links with Jesus. To win that city, however, they had to fight those who ruled the whole area. The famous Saladin (in Arabic, Salah-ad-Din) was a Kurd from Iraq who captured Jerusalem in 1187. He fought and defeated the Crusaders. The Crusades lasted until 1291. The Muslims won, but it left the country fatally weakened in the face of the next invaders—the Mongols.

In 1258, the ferocious Hülegü Khan, grandson of Genghis Khan, and his Mongol warriors reduced Baghdad to rubble and massacred 800,000 people. The story goes that the Tigris River ran red with the blood of Baghdad's inhabitants, then black with ink from the great manuscripts thrown from Mustansiriyyah College, which stood—and still stands—on its banks. Baghdad became part of the huge Mongol Empire.

In 1401, the Mongol leader Tamerlane (Timur the Lame) sacked Baghdad again and massacred many of its inhabitants. By the beginning of the sixteenth century,

"When I lead my army against Baghdad in anger, whether you hide in heaven or in earth I will bring you down from the spinning spheres; I will toss you in the air like a lion. I will leave no one alive in your realm . . ."

—Hülegü Khan's message to the caliph of Baghdad.

▼ *This room is in the beautiful Abbasid Palace in Baghdad, built during the twelfth century during the reign of Caliph Al Nasser Lidnillah. It contains a spacious central courtyard and many delicately carved ceilings.*

Baghdad's population was reduced to 150,000 from a peak of 1 million, and its irrigation system was badly neglected.

▲ *This Persian painting in a book from the fourteenth century illustrates the last stand of Baghdad before it fell to Hülegü Khan. You can clearly see the city walls and the soldiers outside.*

The Ottomans

In 1534, Süleyman the Magnificent, an Ottoman from nearby Turkey, defeated the Mongols. At the height of his powers, he ruled over territory that spread from the deserts of North Africa to the plains of Hungary.

Baghdad was one of the main cities from which the Ottomans ruled their empire. The Ottomans taxed the residents heavily, using the money to support other parts of their empire and neglecting Baghdad itself. Diseases ran through the city, killing a people weakened by lack of food. People began to leave Baghdad and live by herding animals in the countryside.

The Ottomans remained in charge for four hundred years. Mahmud II, who ruled from 1808 to 1839, started reforms in

Baghdad and other parts of the Ottoman Empire. He assumed greater control of the military and restored the power of the central government.

In 1831, the city was attacked again, not by an invader but by the bubonic plague, which killed thousands. Floods ran through the streets that same year, destroying and killing thousands more.

In the late 1860s, Midhat Pasha became governor of Baghdad. He forced landowners to pay taxes, which allowed him to make huge improvements to the city. He pulled down the old city wall, allowing Baghdad to expand, and established a streetcar system, parks, a water system, a hospital, textile mills, a savings bank, and paved and lighted streets. He built the first bridge over the Tigris, opened schools, founded a printing press, set up a steamboat service, and established new municipalities and administrative councils.

British Rule

The discovery of oil at the end of the nineteenth century meant that other countries became interested in a share of Iraq's riches. Great Britain was already a trading partner, buying 65 percent of the goods Iraq produced for export, including oil. In March 1917, during World War I, the British army took Baghdad. They defeated the Ottomans ruling Baghdad, who were supporting the Germans.

In 1918, the Ottoman Empire collapsed as defeated Turkey signed a cease-fire, and

The Orient Express: A Train of Mystery

The British built the impressive Mosul-Baghdad-Damascus railway and the railroad line that linked Baghdad to Istanbul. Baghdad became the second-to-last stop for the train known as the Orient Express. The novelist Agatha Christie wrote Murder on the Orient Express *while a long-time resident at the Baghdad Hotel, which housed many of her belongings until looted after the war in late 2003.*

the Allies divided up the Arab lands among themselves. France kept Syria, Lebanon, and some of northern Iraq while Britain controlled the southern half of the country, promising "liberation not occupation." In 1921, there was an election for king; 96 percent of the population were said to have voted, but the results were rigged. The British crowned Faisal I as a puppet king.

The British did not want Iraq to be independent because they wanted to control its precious oil. They used any means, including shooting people without trial and poisonous phosphorous bombs, against anyone who rose up against them. Britain's Winston Churchill, at that time a minister in its government, argued in favor of using "poison gas against uncivilized tribes to spread a lively terror." The Iraqis resisted the British, blowing up the pipelines carrying the oil and thus forcing the British to give up control of the oil fields.

Iraq in the Mid-1900s

When the British finally left in 1932 and Iraq became independent, the average life expectancy for Iraqis was only twenty-six years. Only 10 percent of the population could read.

Since foreigners were doing many jobs, many Iraqis were unemployed. King Faisal died in 1933 and was succeeded by his son Ghazi, who died in 1939. Ghazi's son, Faisal II, then inherited the throne.

▼ *Men wear traditional outfits on this crowded street in Baghdad in the 1920s. There are no women on the street; in those days, women mostly stayed at home.*

During World War II, Iraq again sided with Germany, this time as a way of getting rid of the British whom many Iraqis felt were still in charge. Despite promising support, the Germans never came to Iraq, and the British reached Baghdad. Winston Churchill, now Britain's prime minister, congratulated British troops and noted that "the immediate task is to get a friendly government set up in Baghdad."

Saddam Hussein and Oil

In 1943, a political group called the Ba'ath (Resurrection) Party was set up in Syria; its aim was to bring all the Arab nations together. Saddam Hussein Takriti became a member of the Ba'ath Party in 1956, when he was about twenty years old, and quickly became powerful. The last king of Iraq, Faisal II, ruled until 1958, when the Iraqi army executed him and proclaimed Iraq an independent nation. Brigadier General Abdul Karim Kassem led the country until 1963, when members of the Ba'ath Party and Arab nationalists seized control. Various powers took over the country until 1979, when Saddam Hussein became president.

The Perils of Petroleum

All Iraqis, from ministers to shoe shine boys, say, "Oil is both our blessing and our curse." Oil has brought the country riches, but it has also brought those who seek to conquer to get their hands on the "black gold," as oil is sometimes called.

During the early 1970s, Iraq's government, led by the Ba'athists, took control of the country's oil industry from private companies. The oil boom of the 1970s brought wealth to Baghdad, and the city was developed on an impressive scale.

When Saddam Hussein became president of Iraq, he had hundreds of politicians and army leaders, whom he suspected were opponents, killed immediately. One of his first actions as president, however, was to pour money into water purification, housing, education, and other improvements for Baghdad, investing $5 million in one hospital complex alone. With Saddam's use of the money from oil, Baghdad grew into a bustling modern city. Unfortunately, he also became a ruthless and cruel dictator. His secret police tortured thousands; his control of the courts was absolute; and few who opposed him in any way got a fair trial. By the end of his rule, over two hundred thousand Iraqis had been killed.

In 1980, Saddam Hussein led his country into a war with Iran in a dispute over the Shatt al Arab waterway that runs along the border between the two countries and over who controlled the Persian Gulf. Saddam also feared that Iran, which had become a religious state, would encourage an uprising in Iraq against its secular (nonreligious) government. The West, including Britain and the United States, supported Saddam against Iran at this time. By the time the war ended in

"Under a dictatorship you don't have the right to anything, no freedom to choose, no opportunities. If you are poor you cannot be a doctor or a student. Everybody is afraid. People who are against the government, they disappear."

—Amani, an Iraqi refugee, in February 2003.

1988, more than 1 million people had died and 1.5 million were left homeless in the two countries.

Saddam Hussein continued to prohibit people from expressing their opinions against him and killed many thousands of people who did not agree with him. In 1988, he ordered the army to use conventional and chemical bombs for three days on Halabja, a Kurdish town of seventy thousand people located about 150 miles (241 km) northeast of Baghdad. Many thousands of people died, including women and children.

The Gulf War and Sanctions

In 1990, Iraq accused neighboring Kuwait of stealing oil by drilling under the Iraq border and taking Iraq's land. Negotiations failed, and Iraq invaded Kuwait. Many countries, including the U.S., came together to remove the Iraqi invaders in what was called the Gulf War. Although the war ended with a cease-fire agreement in 1991, troubles for the people of Baghdad and Iraq did not.

▲ *During the time he was president, Saddam Hussein's image was everywhere—painted with a telephone on the central telephone exchange, in military dress outside a soldiers' barracks, and in every school, hospital, or public building. Here, his picture appears on a post office building.*

▲ In March 2003, smoke covered the compound of one of the presidential palaces in Baghdad during a massive air raid led by the United States on the Iraqi capital.

When Saddam Hussein attacked Kuwait, the United Nations (UN) imposed what are known as sanctions, which means the country was not allowed to buy from or sell goods to other countries. If Iraq had no income, the UN believed, it not afford the weapons for another war. The sanctions led to great hardships for the people of Baghdad and other Iraqis, however, who did not have enough food to eat. Many people died. In response to this human tragedy, the United Nations oil-for-food program was agreed upon in 1995, but it was not until 1997 that a limited number of goods began to enter the country. Food imports increased, while medical supplies and health care services improved somewhat. Living standards remained far below the levels of 1990, however, when the sanctions were imposed.

The Second Iraq War
In 2003, a coalition made up primarily of U.S. and British troops invaded Iraq to get

rid of Saddam Hussein and to find the dangerous weapons that they thought he had hidden to use against the United States and other nations. They called the invasion "Operation Iraqi Freedom." The U.S. government also claimed that Saddam was linked to al Qaeda, the terrorist organization responsible for attacks on the World Trade Center in New York and the Pentagon in Washington, D.C., on September 11, 2001.

Troops found Saddam Hussein, but they did not find the weapons. The U.S. Central Intelligence Agency concluded that Iraq stopped producing these weapons in 1991. A U.S. commission later found Saddam had not collaborated with al Qaeda on the September 11 attacks. Many experts believe that the war was really about control of Iraq's oil. In June 2004, an acting government advised by the U.S. was set up. The American and British troops remained.

The 2005 Elections
Weeks of escalating violence preceded the national elections, held on January 30, 2005. Information on candidates and on where to vote was difficult to obtain; telephones, faxes, cell phones, and the Internet were disconnected. Many people stayed away from the elections because of threats on their lives. Most Iraqis are Muslims and belong to either the Sunni or Shiite sect (*see page 20*). Although the majority of Iraqis are Shiites, for many years the government had been dominated by Sunnis, the more secular of the two groups. Some Sunnis, now fearful

"Since when are Iraqis afraid of anything? We don't have time for fear . . . We're ready for anything. Right now, as I'm talking, a mortar could just fall and kill us."

—Mohammed Abbas, supermarket owner, talking about the determination of many Iraqis to vote in the 2005 elections, despite intimidation.

of rule under the more traditional Shiites, called for a boycott of the elections. Although the elections had the support of the U.S. and the UN, some international law experts believed they were illegal according to the Geneva and Vienna Conventions, since foreign armies occupied the country.

Despite all these issues, an estimated 58 percent of voters turned out, braving the dangers of the streets. The newly elected members of the National Assembly met on March 16, 2005. Choosing a new president and prime minister proved to be a very difficult task. The Kurdish leader Jalal Talabani was finally chosen as president, with two vice-presidents, Adel Abdul Mahdi, a Shiite, and Ghazi Yawar, a Sunni, to assist him. In April, Iraqi Shiite leader Ibrahim al Jaafari was named prime minister of the country's new interim government, at least until the December 2005 elections. In the meantime, Iraqi civilians and U.S. and allied soldiers, including many Iraqi troops, continue to suffer assaults from insurgents and die on a daily basis.

CHAPTER 2

People of Baghdad

The population of Baghdad has grown quickly over the last fifty years. In 1932, under British rule, Baghdad's population was recorded as 358,840. It is now estimated at over 6 million.

Life and Death

Baghdad, like many other cities in the Middle East, is mainly a city of young people. Almost half the population is under the age of eighteen, and only 3 percent of the population is over sixty-five. The children of Iraq are caught up in war for the third time in twenty years; anyone under the age of twenty has never lived in a time of peace, making it hard for young people to imagine what normal life would be like.

Life in Baghdad was very hard in the fourteen years between the two wars in Iraq. Jobs paid badly—with no trade, there were few of them—and many people did not have enough to eat. Until 1990, Baghdadis enjoyed a good health care system and good education, but under sanctions, people had to learn to live with very little. In Iraq as a whole, from 1990 to 2003, approximately 1.5 million children died due to lack of food and other factors. In 2005, seven out of ten children suffered

◀ *These Baghdadi families are gathered outside the Kadhimain Shrine, one of many old and beautiful mosques in the city.*

◄ This child in the Sadr City Hospital is suffering from dehydration. This condition is often caused by diarrhea, which people get from drinking dirty water—the result of the destruction of the water systems during the 2003 war.

from various degrees of diarrhea, because the war had destroyed the water system. UN sanctions denied the country parts for repair, resulting in poor sanitation.

Estimates of Iraqi deaths since the war began in 2003 range from 25,000 to 100,000. Violence accounted for most of these deaths, including attacks by insurgents and air coalition forces.

A Melting Pot

Because it has been invaded so many times, Baghdad's people are a mixture of Arabs, Kurds from the north, a small Jewish community, and Turkomans from Turkmenistan, Afghanistan, and Iran. Most people are Muslims, but there are also different denominations of Christians, such as the Chaldeans. Before the Gulf War and sanctions, many migrant workers also lived in

Baghdad, including Afghans, Pakistanis, Palestinians, Indians, and Somalis.

Arabic is the official language in Baghdad. Many educated people have been to school in Great Britain or the United States and also speak English.

Religion: Islam Dominates

Baghdad has been a Muslim city since its beginnings in 762. Over 95 percent of all Iraqis follow the religion of Islam. Islam's God is called Allah, the Creator, and his prophet, the founder of the religion, is Muhammad. Muslims' holy book is the

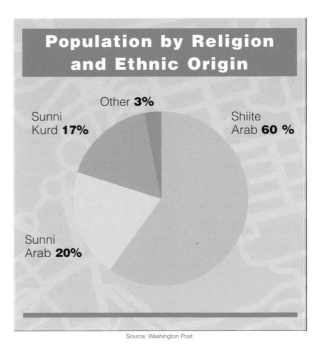

Population by Religion and Ethnic Origin

Sunni Kurd **17%**

Other **3%**

Shiite Arab **60 %**

Sunni Arab **20%**

Source: Washington Post

▲ *Shiite Muslims take part in Friday prayers at the Mussa al Kazem mosque in the Kazemiya district of Baghdad. In Islam, men and women pray separately.*

Koran (or Qur'an). Islam is a way of life. Clothes, body, and community must be spotlessly clean; worshipers must wash their faces, hands, arms, and feet before praying five times a day. Muslims believe they have a duty dictated by Allah to look after each other.

Muslims are divided into two main sects, the Sunnis and the Shiites. Their differences date back to the seventh century, when the Prophet Muhammad died, and are more political than religious. Shiites believe that the leader of the Muslims should be someone descended from Muhammad's family. Upon Muhammad's death, they followed his cousin, Ali ibn Abi Talib. Sunnis believe that the community should choose the most qualified Muslim to be their leader; they supported Abu Bakr, a close companion of the Prophet Muhammad, when Muhammad died. Shiites make up less than 10 percent of world's

Muslims, although they are more than half the Muslim population of Iraq. Sunnis include both Arabs and Kurds. Under Saddam Hussein, many of those in power in Baghdad were Sunni. The new government is trying to have a balance between Sunnis, Shiites, and the Kurds from the north of the country.

Where People Worship

Baghdad has always been a city of many religions, with mosques, shrines, churches, and two synagogues. With their golden domes and turquoise mosaics, the mosques glitter in the sun. Famous mosques include the Al Gailani, named after a scholar who lived, taught, and contemplated there until his death in 1165. The great Al Imam Al

The Many Uses of Mosques

Mosques are not only for praying. They are practical as well as religious places. In times of war, people shelter there, and the buildings provide collection points for blood, medicine, and aid. In times of peace, scholars and civic groups hold their meetings in mosques. Mosque leaders often provide political advice to their followers and urge political action. For example, some clerics asked their followers not to participate in the elections of January 2005.

Adham Mosque was originally built in 1066 at the site of a famous shrine. Like Baghdad itself, it has been destroyed and rebuilt many times since then. The Caliph's Mosque near the animal market is modern, but the minaret attached to it is one thousand years old.

Baghdad boasts many churches, too, most of them built in the 1800s. The Roman Catholic Church was completed in 1866 on the site of a chapel to Saint Thomas. Other churches include the Armenian Orthodox Church of the Virgin Mary, the Chaldean Catholic Church, and the Syriac Catholic Church of the Virgin Mary.

Festivals

Under Saddam Hussein, Iraq was a secular (nonreligious) country, and people followed their own religious customs. Muslims would celebrate Ramadan and Eid al Fitr, and Christians would celebrate Christmas.

▼ *As part of the religious Shiite festival of Ashura, these actors in Baghdad are re-enacting the battle of Kerbala, in which Imam Hussein, grandson of the Prophet Muhammad, was killed.*

Ramadan is the most important religious festival for Muslims. It falls in the ninth month of the Muslim calendar. Muslims eat and drink before daylight and fast until after dark to concentrate on spiritual matters. The evening meal each day is a celebration with family, friends, and special foods. Ramadan ends with three days of holiday called Eid al Fitr, when children receive new clothes, and presents are exchanged. In Baghdad today, however, few people can afford to buy presents; this feels to many somewhat like a birthday being canceled. Other Muslim holidays celebrate the birthday of the Prophet Muhammad or the beginning of the Islamic New Year.

Under Saddam Hussein's government, the country also celebrated a number of holidays that were based on historical or military events. These included July Revolution Day on July 17 that celebrated the Ba'ath Party's return to power in 1968. After the 2003 war, Iraq's first post-war governing council canceled this together with other holidays associated with Saddam's rule. Iraq's new government may now decide to institute some new public holidays instead.

Food and Hospitality

Between 1990 and 2003, many people, even doctors and teachers, depended on food handouts from the government because they earned so little money. Today, an estimated sixty percent of Iraqis still depend

Party Time

Baghdad is arguably the spice capital of the world; you can smell the cooking aromas well before the dishes are served. For a party, a meal might consist of:

- Djaj belkari: *Baked chicken casserole with numerous seasonal vegetables and topped with browned potatoes, spices, and tomato paste*
- Kosi: *A whole lamb stuffed with almonds, raisins, and spices*
- Dolme: *Grapevine leaves filled with an array of red lentils, parsley, mint, tomatoes, spices, and cloves, wrapped into a neat packet, and baked*
- Mezze: *These appetizers always cover the table, so many and so complicated that a foreigner might assume this is the meal rather than the appetizer. Mezze may include* tabbouleh, *which is cracked wheat soaked in lime or lemon juice and oil, mixed with finely chopped parsley, mint, tomatoes, garlic, and onion; falafel, a kind of dumpling made with ground chickpeas; numerous salads with different ingredients; hummus, a delicious dip of mashed chickpeas; and/or baba ghanoush, made of chilled, cooked, pureed eggplant. Hummus and baba ghanoush are both eaten with great rounds of pungent, hot, flat bread placed in piles around the table.*

on these handouts, but this support is not enough to live on and poor families suffer. Children are not getting enough to eat; many are underweight, undernourished, or suffer from the effects of malnutrition.

▲ The family pictured here is eating the evening meal, called iftar, during Ramadan, when eating is forbidden between sunrise and sunset.

Four ingredients are very important to the varied flavors of Iraqi cooking: fresh mint, parsley, thick tomato paste, and a tangy, thick yogurt made from the milk of water buffaloes. Rice is also a staple for Iraqis as is thick, dark, bitter coffee and scented golden tea served in tiny glasses.

Women do all the cooking. During the sanctions and since the 2003 war, electrical supplies have been haphazard. Women have had to cook on kerosene burners; this has led to many deaths and injuries when clothes caught fire or burners exploded.

Hospitality in Baghdad is very special. To admire something in a home, be it food, a piece of jewelry, or a beautiful cup, is to be instantly told it is yours.

"Eat together—do not eat separately, for the blessing is with the company."

—Iraqi saying.

Feasting on Fish

The fish restaurants along the banks of the Tigris have opened again, but as fighting continues, few people dare to go there. The fish come from special artificial lakes just outside Baghdad, where they are fed an exact diet to give them the best flavor when cooked in the traditional Iraqi manner called mazgoof. *The fish are speared with a stick that is then stuck into the ground to cook by fire. Before the war, people would come and eat at the restaurants until four in the morning; they were always crowded. During the war, much of the city was reduced to rubble, but now some rebuilding has begun. Municipal workers have planted trees and bushes, and the owners of the fish restaurants hope customers will soon return.*

CHAPTER 3

Living in Baghdad

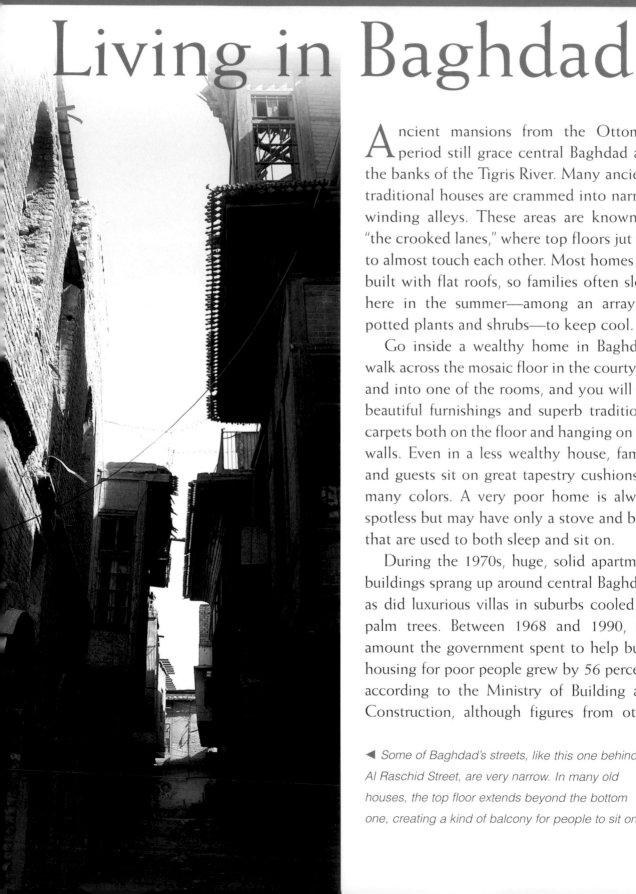

Ancient mansions from the Ottoman period still grace central Baghdad and the banks of the Tigris River. Many ancient, traditional houses are crammed into narrow winding alleys. These areas are known as "the crooked lanes," where top floors jut out to almost touch each other. Most homes are built with flat roofs, so families often sleep here in the summer—among an array of potted plants and shrubs—to keep cool.

Go inside a wealthy home in Baghdad, walk across the mosaic floor in the courtyard and into one of the rooms, and you will see beautiful furnishings and superb traditional carpets both on the floor and hanging on the walls. Even in a less wealthy house, family and guests sit on great tapestry cushions of many colors. A very poor home is always spotless but may have only a stove and beds that are used to both sleep and sit on.

During the 1970s, huge, solid apartment buildings sprang up around central Baghdad, as did luxurious villas in suburbs cooled by palm trees. Between 1968 and 1990, the amount the government spent to help build housing for poor people grew by 56 percent, according to the Ministry of Building and Construction, although figures from other

◄ *Some of Baghdad's streets, like this one behind Al Raschid Street, are very narrow. In many old houses, the top floor extends beyond the bottom one, creating a kind of balcony for people to sit on.*

sources differ. Since the war began in 2003, however, subsidized housing has ceased, and rents have become unaffordable for many. Some people have been evicted from their homes, and whole families have sought shelter in bombed buildings, factories, or mosques, or they have made shelters of whatever they could find.

Water, Sanitation, and Electricity

Many sanitation and water facilities were destroyed by the war and then looted. This damage means that the sewage from the whole city is being discharged into the Tigris River. Half the sewage plants are now working again, but hundreds of thousands of tons of raw and partially treated sewage pour into the rivers every day. Even when sewage plants have been rebuilt, insurgents have tried to destroy them again.

The electricity system was also badly bombed and looted. Some people pulled down pylons to take valuable copper from the wires. Today, only half the needed electricity supply is available. Unless they can afford private generators, many people have only a few hours of electricity a day.

Education

Before 1990, "the education system in Iraq was considered one of the best in the region," according to the World Bank. From 1974 onward, children in Iraq could attend school for free from kindergarten through college. After college, the government would pay for them to study in foreign countries. Regardless of their wealth or background, if they had the ability, young people could train for any profession they wished.

After Iraq became a republic in 1958, girls were also expected to go to school. Before then, as in many developing countries today, families considered it more important to educate boys, whom they believed would support their future families financially, than to educate girls. The educational situation

Sadr City

The most densely populated part of Baghdad is Sadr City (left), home to 2 million people. Their houses, or shabby apartment buildings, are often too close for someone to squeeze between. Many look out onto wasteland. Sometimes, as many as twenty people live in two rooms. The media often refer to the area as a slum. It is certainly very poor, but residents who have a bit more often share with those who do not, so there is a sense of a close-knit society despite the obvious poverty.

▲ *Mohammed Assad (left) at the Al Mithak Elementary school in Baghdad. The black scarf on the desk is in memory of his friend Akil who was killed in an explosion in 2004 along with forty other people, most of them children.*

has changed a lot in just one generation: Many educated women today have mothers who never went to school.

In 1978, the government organized a campaign to teach every person between the ages of fifteen and forty-five to read. A year later, Iraq won an international award for promoting literacy in this program. Under Saddam Hussein, young people benefited from a good education, although all students had to learn the president's version of Iraq history. After the war in 2003, course books were rewritten by a team of U.S.-appointed Iraqi educators.

Since the 1980s, war, international sanctions, and lack of funding have severely damaged the educational system. After the Gulf War, about 50 percent of the schools in Baghdad were no longer useable; they had been destroyed, looted, or were just falling apart. The sanctions meant that toys, paper, blackboards, and textbooks were not allowed into the country. Many teachers left for better-paid jobs.

An Iraqi government survey in early 2004 said that since the invasion in March 2003, bombs had damaged over seven hundred Iraqi primary schools, more than two hundred schools had been burned, and over three thousand had been looted. Over a third of these were in Baghdad.

Although the law requires children between the ages of six and twelve to attend school, nearly one in four children do not—

"When a man proposes marriage, the woman's family's first question is not his job, or income even, but 'What did he do his degree on?'"

—Sana al Khayyat in *Honour and Shame: Women in Modern Iraq,* 1990.

31 percent of girls and 17 percent of boys. Many children—and their parents—do not feel it is safe to leave their homes. Children at schools have been kidnapped and held for ransom, and attackers have entered schools. Girls are particularly at risk of violence. Also, families often need their children's income from any work they can find or do not have enough money for school clothes and supplies. Universities, whose students had been equally divided between male and female before the 2003 war began, lost many female students since it became harder for women to safely leave their homes.

Schools and Universities

There are more than one thousand primary schools, hundreds of intermediate and secondary schools, and three universities in Baghdad. Officially, children ages five through eleven are required to attend primary school. They then go to intermediate school until the age of fourteen and have to pass a test to enter secondary school. At secondary school, students follow a baccalaureate system where they take examinations in a wide range of subjects. At seventeen, they either go to work or begin studying at universities or vocational and technical schools.

Baghdad is the most important center of learning in Iraq, boasting the University of Baghdad (established in 1957) and the University of Technology (established in 1974). The current Al Mustansiriyya University was established in 1963, but the Mustansiriyya College itself dates back to the thirteenth century. Now there are a number of private colleges, but rising tuition fees are making it difficult for students to continue with their studies.

Shopping

Because the United Nations did not allow products other than essential foods and medicines into the country, the years of sanctions largely destroyed Baghdad's modern shopping districts. In about 1998, however, neighboring countries, saddened by Iraq's plight, began to defy the sanctions.

Ice Cream Day

Like many Baghdadis, Maithan Maki finds that his world since 2003 war began has been turned upside down. That is why he takes his family out for ice cream on a hot summer night, trying to keep things normal. "Friday is just for the family, and coming here for ice cream is something we've always done," says Mr. Maki, accompanied by his wife and two small daughters. "We aren't going to give it up because of dangers or the economic situation."

Designer clothes from Paris, London, Milan, and New York were on sale again in sparkling, sophisticated shops in the central shopping districts of Kadhimiya, Kharamha, and Karrada. About the same time, art galleries and stores selling fine Iraqi jewelry—gold is cheap and of luminous red, ocher, and white—sprang back to life.

Iraq has a tradition of exquisite handmade clothing; tailors can copy anything from a sketch or magazine and deliver the dress or suit the next day. As fine fabrics again emerged on the market, many Baghdadis preferred to buy their clothing this way.

▼ *Souk al Sarabady is one of Baghdad's many indoor markets in the Kazemiyah district. Each market specializes in a certain type of goods; al Sarabady sells clothing and material.*

In Baghdad, as in most Middle Eastern cities, different shopping areas serve specific needs. In one area, you can fix a car and buy parts, choosing from many different garages. Another area specializes in computers, another in furniture, children's toys, or groceries. Shops are usually family owned.

The Animal and Book Markets

The closest Baghdad has to a shopping mall are the ancient souks, or markets, in their dimly lit alleys. Displays of nuts of every flavor and hue, dried or fresh fruit, and vegetables arranged according to color dazzle shoppers. Many souks have their own specialty—intricate copperware, carpets in rich colors, or handicrafts. Above all the bustle wafts the smell of fresh coffee, of cardamom, and of tiny glasses of tea

▶ *Iraqis make their way through the rush hour traffic in July 2004, near the popular Al Shorja Market in central Baghdad July 2004. The market is one of the oldest in Baghdad and sells all kinds of goods.*

flavored with different herbs. The poor and many of the middle class buy their food and clothing in the souks.

On Fridays, after prayers, the two oldest markets in the Middle East bustle and hustle. The animal market in the Shorja district in central Baghdad lies in the shadow of the Caliph's Mosque. Everything is for sale—from a lynx to a lark, snakes to schnauzers. Birds in colors of translucent jewels preen in impossibly exotic cages made from palm fronds. In the dusty back streets among ancient ruins, cocks fight in bloody battles for their owners, despite laws forbidding cockfights.

Nearby, the Al Muntanabi Street book market winds through ancient, open alleys and dusky, covered walkways. Books are displayed on the ground, in piles on shelves from floor to ceiling, and in trunks or boxes under wobbly tables. Precious books often are hidden under the vendor's clothing. The market's origins are said to go back to the time of the first caliphs, the rulers after the death of Muhammad in the seventh century. A Middle East saying proclaims, "Books are written in Egypt, printed in Lebanon, and read in Iraq." Books from *Harry Potter* to *Artemis Fowl*, from ancient texts to modern novels, on topics from long-dead civilizations to space-age exploration—and the equivalent in a dozen languages—can be found here.

Transportation

Baghdad's now-battered transportation system has a proud, often complex history. Germany paid for the railway system in the early 1900s, and Britain completed the central railway station with its magnificent dome in 1948. This network connects Mosul in northern Iraq to Basra in the south and Baghdad and Damascus, Syria, to Istanbul in Turkey. Bombed in 1991, the railway system is now in a sad state.

Before the Gulf War, the bustling marble-halled airport hosted most of the world's national carriers. It was bombed but reopened in 1998.

In normal times, buses carry travelers through the desert to Jordan, Syria, Turkey, and Iran. In Baghdad, most buses are old and spew pollution, although in recent years, a few modern ones have been imported from India. Official taxis are orange and white, unbelievably cheap, and very battered. There are also the unofficial taxis. As unemployment and inflation have spiraled, it often seems as if every Iraqi uses the family car as a means of income. It is not unusual to find your driver was once an airline pilot, a ship's captain, an engineer—even a doctor or university professor. "Baghdad must be the only place on earth where your driver will ask you if you happen to have a CD of Brahms or Beethoven, or a copy of some obscure academic volume," commented one senior United Nations official.

Before the war in 2003, most people traveled in cars, which in rush hour were backed up along the main highways. Today, however, because of continuing insurgent attacks and fighting between soldiers and rebels, many people are too frightened to go out, and lines for gas can last two days.

The Environment

War is dangerous in more than just the obvious ways. Bombings and attacks can leave many poisons in the environment. The residue from bombed factories and dangerous industries, like fertilizer plants or car factories, can make people ill. After the 1991 Gulf War, thousands of Iraqis and their children, together with U.S., British, and other soldiers in the region, became sick. Many of these people have never recovered. The war that began in 2003 has resulted in even more bombings and

Garbage Plagues Baghdad Slum

For years, an empty plot in Al Hurya had been a dumping ground for the capital's construction companies. Now, however, along with the bricks and tiles, mounds of household garbage are being dumped on this 60-square-yard (50-square-meter) patch of wasteland, which lies between Al Hurya and the wealthier Al Adil neighborhood. Fifteen-year-old Akeel Mahdi sells fruit on the main road into Al Hurya near the ever-expanding garbage dump. He says the sight and smell of the rotting refuse is starting to repulse customers and affect his sales. "The garbage trucks dump loads there everyday. The municipality cleans the place up from time to time, but it's pretty pointless because they just come back again. Until the authorities find a way to stop them, it's just going to keep getting worse," he said.

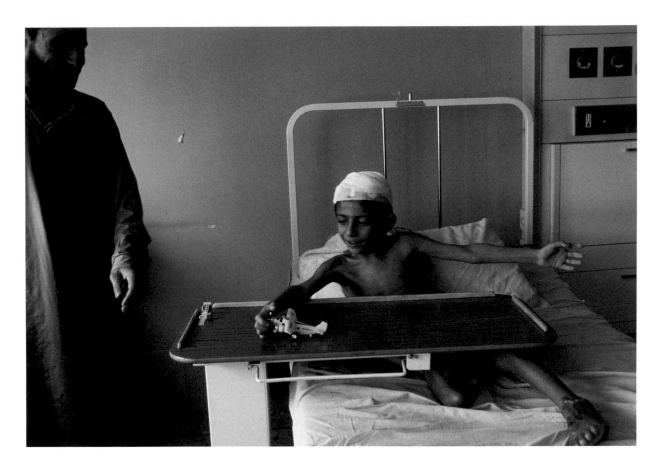

▲ *Salam, pictured here in Baghdad Medical City Surgical Hospital, was injured during bombing when an electric cable hit him. Doctors had to amputate his leg.*

damage. Many doctors and scientists are worried that this time even more people may become ill.

Dangers for Children

Children face many environmental dangers in Baghdad today. Water is not clean, and illnesses, many fatal, result. In Baghdad, the war has damaged about 40 percent of the water and sewage pipeline network. The lines supplying fuel for sewage-treatment facilities have broken down, so those plants are not operating. Plants have been looted. Equipment and qualified people to maintain that equipment are no longer available.

Children are also at risk from unexploded bombs. An estimated eight hundred dangerous sites dot Baghdad alone; the majority contains cluster bombs and caches of dumped ammunition. Children are injured or killed on a daily basis when playing on or near these sites.

In the summer, food spoils very quickly. Electricity for refrigerators is unreliable, however, so many people suffer from stomach problems from spoiled food.

Chapter 4

Baghdad at Work

Iraq should be a rich country. It contains the world's second-largest reserves of oil, and oil used to provide 95 percent of its earnings from other countries. It was also the world's largest exporter of dates. Three wars in the last twenty years have made it poor, however.

For centuries, Baghdad had been the richest and economically most important city of Iraq. The city had a wide variety of industries producing leather goods, furniture, wood products, chemicals, electrical equipment, clothing, bricks, cement, tobacco, and beverages. Oil refineries, food-processing plants, tanneries, and textile mills spread throughout Baghdad. It was also the center of the country's financial operations and the headquarters of the Central Bank of Iraq. Most of the national government administration is located here, and the state is still the main employer in Baghdad.

National Government

Saddam Hussein, as president, head of state, head of the army and the ruling Ba'ath party, had all the power in the country before the 2003 war. He picked the people he wanted to be in charge and few people dared question him. Saddam ruled by means of a Revolutionary Command Council (RCC)

◄ *Hadji Abbas, pictured here, has his shop in the old Thafafin souk in Baghdad, where many other tailors ply their trade.*

that was in charge of all laws and commanded the military.

Under the RCC, the National Assembly held 250 elected members who represented various political and social groups, but Saddam controlled the elections and the assembly's decisions.

After the war in 2003, Saddam's government was replaced by the U.S.-led Coalition Provisional Authority (CPA), which handed over power to an Iraqi Interim government in 2004, formed to rule until the elections had taken place in January 2005. Voters then elected 275 members to the Transitional National Assembly. The assembly appointed a Presidential Council consisting of a president (whose role is mainly ceremonial) and two vice-presidents. The assembly had to approve the presidential council's choice of prime minister—Ibrahim al Jaafari—and his choice of cabinet ministers. This cabinet was dominated by Shiites but included Sunni Arab and Kurdish politicians. Some think it is not a good idea to pick people because of the community or religion they belong to, but it has been difficult to find another way to ensure that everyone is fairly represented.

The new government's main task is now to draft a new Iraqi constitution—the rules and principles by which Iraq will be governed. This draft will then be put to the public vote. If the draft constitution is approved, the government must then prepare Iraq for another election in December 2005 to elect a permanent government.

Local Government

Iraq is divided into eighteen governorates, which resemble states or provinces. Baghdad is one of these. Each province is divided into districts, and these are in turn divided into subdistricts. Baghdad is made up of nine districts.

Before 2003, a governor nominated by the central government ran each governorate. In 1972, the Ba'ath party formed Local People's Councils throughout the country, including Baghdad, to give local organizations input to the national government on a variety of issues.

By the time of the January 2005 elections, new councils had been set up throughout the country. Local councils select a few of their members to represent the neighborhood in district councils. The district councils select one or two people to represent them on the city council. Each provincial council has forty-one members, except for Baghdad, which has fifty-one. Councils are supposed to have representation from men and women and from all Iraq's religious groups. These councils represent the people's opinions and needs to the government and now also play a leading role in the reconstruction of their own communities.

Work in Baghdad

Iraq's earnings from exports nearly doubled between 1968 and 1980. Then came the eight-year Iran-Iraq war. The economy still grew during this time, however, and personal incomes rose dramatically. Agriculture, communication, transportation, trade, tourism, the medical sector, and social services all expanded. Many new buildings and hospitals were built. Investment in education increased dramatically; the number of preschools grew by 68 percent, and other educational institutions grew by up to 442 percent.

Before sanctions began in 1991, Baghdad boasted a growing financial market, a stock market, manufacturing, tourism, and Iraq's own international airline. It was also a rapidly expanding city, with engineers, architects, skilled builders, and artisans of every discipline. Many government officials, doctors, teachers, and academics had studied in the United States or Great Britain.

Since the war in 2003, however, the Iraqi economy has shrunk by 22 percent. Only 12 percent of the country's industrial capacity is currently being used.

It is very difficult today to say how many people in Baghdad are working. Unemployment estimates range from 50 to 70 percent. The fact that it is dangerous to go out, particularly for women, makes it

▼ These unemployed Iraqis are training at a Baghdad unemployment center. In early 2005, some organizations estimated that at least half the population of Iraq was unemployed.

*"The majority of Iraqis are . . .
jobless, penniless, and dependent
on UN food handouts."*

—*Washington Post*, August 28, 2003

difficult to get to work. There is no system of government benefits for the unemployed, and sixty percent of the population depends on food rations from the government. The people who do work are not well paid. Most workers in Iraq today earn the equivalent of $60 a month, a small percentage earn $120 a month, and a tiny minority, mostly administrators and managers, make $180.

The working day for those who are employed in Baghdad is from 7:30 A.M. to 2:00 P.M. and then again in the evening. Workers go home for a late lunch and to rest and then go back to work. Shops also close in the afternoon and open again in the evening, particularly in the summer months when it is very hot.

▲ *Zakia Hakki is Iraq's first female judge. She was appointed in 1959, when women and men were made equal under law. She left Iraq in 1996 but came back after the 2003 war as an advisor to the Ministry of Justice. She returned to the U.S. in 2004 for medical treatment following an attempt to assassinate her.*

Women

Baghdadi women have been among the most advanced and freest in terms of education and rights in the Middle East. By 1980, Iraqi women could vote and run for election. In comparison, in Saudi Arabia today on Iraq's southwestern border, women are not even allowed to go out alone; a man must accompany a woman on the street. Under Saddam Hussein, women held senior positions in Baghdad's government, universities, and hospitals. Since the war, however, the poor security situation in Baghdad has made it difficult for women to go out at all, let alone go to work. There has been a huge increase in kidnappings and violent crime, particularly against women, and there are Islamic fundamentalists who are prepared to attack women for not wearing the veil. The future of women in Iraq is uncertain: Parliament is putting together a new constitution, and some people fear that women's rights will not be included.

CHAPTER 5

Baghdad at Play

Although many children have become fearful because of the war and the following insurgency, they continue to play games, hold soccer matches, and tell stories, snatching a moment of fun when they can. Traditions of picnics beside the Tigris and weekend outings has nearly stopped, but people still remember those times.

Children at Play

Computers and computer games are now available in Baghdad, but most people cannot afford them. So for children, traditional games and their own imagination are still the main ways to amuse themselves. They play hopscotch or another game resembling jacks that involves throwing a small stone in the air and seeing how many other stones can be picked up before the falling stone is caught. They often spend hours making intricate miniature houses, arches, and bridges from matchsticks, matchboxes, and even soft metal lids that can be bent and shaped. They also fashion models and designs from paper—an Iraqi form of Japan's delicate art of

◄ *Baghdad's Symphony Orchestra, pictured here, used to be famous throughout the Middle East. During the sanctions of the 1990s, it was very difficult for them to practice because they could not obtain new music or parts for their instruments. Now that the war is over, the orchestra hopes to revive itself and it has played in both Baghdad and Washington D.C.*

Soccer, Baghdad-style

On a dusty field in the heart of war-torn Baghdad, scores of Iraqi children are playing soccer and dreaming that one day they will become stars of the national team. "I love Iraq," says five-year-old Amir Hussein as he practices with friends on the soccer field on Abu al Nawas Street, a once-popular promenade on the banks of the Tigris River, now deserted. Amir shares the same ambition as the rest of the 120 children who gather for weekly training on a playing field that was once reserved for the security agents of Saddam Hussein. Concerned parents in Baghdad's Al Karada neighborhood formed the free training school to give hope to the city's children amid the daily diet of insurgent bombings, kidnappings, and counterattacks. A charity donates balls, shirts, and shoes for the players.

"My grandparents had a house by the Tigris. We used to go out on a boat from their house. It was quite a beautiful and gentle place . . . the whole family used to gather there for lunch . . . . That is a very important part of Iraqi social life, that if anyone comes you make them a feast. That's really not possible now."

—Maysoon Pachachi, Iraqi filmmaker, February 3, 2003.

origami. Swimming is a passion, performed in the tributaries, lakes, and great rivers. In Baghdad, a city divided by the Tigris and spanned by great bridges, the young climb up the vast pillars that hold the bridges to a platform halfway up, then dive into the river.

Story Time

Iraqis love telling stories and have always done so. Many of the stories that children around the world love so much come from the region that is now Iraq. Sinbad the Sailor, it is said, came from Basra, Iraq's second largest city. He is part of the stories of *One Thousand and One Nights* that have been handed down from parent to child for more than a thousand years. In Iraq during the tenth century, al Jahshiyari first compiled and wrote down the stories. He added tales from local storytellers to an old Persian work, *Hazar Afsana* (A Thousand Tales), which in turn contained some stories of Indian origin.

The Weekend

The real weekend begins on Thursday afternoon because Friday is the Muslim Sabbath. The week begins again on Saturday. Friday is for visiting relatives and friends, including departed loved ones in the cemeteries. When it is safe, is also a day for family outings, picnics, or a visit to Baghdad's famous zoo, set in acres of lush palms. In peaceful times, Baghdadis enjoyed a trip on a riverboat or a visit to the island of Tajaiyat in the Tigris north of Baghdad, with its lake, swimming pools, tennis courts, playgrounds, restaurants, rowing boats, and outdoor movies. Iraqis are passionate about

The Race Returns

Iraq's first horse races started in 1920 under British rule and have been held three times a week almost every season since, despite wars and invasions. The Baghdad Equestrian Club flourished under Saddam Hussein, whose sons Uday and Qusay and his half-brother Barzan al Tikriti all owned horses that were never allowed to lose a race. Today, whatever is happening elsewhere in Baghdad, the races continue.

"The situation today has affected all parts of life in Iraq, except the races. Here life is normal," says Sheikh Juma'a Mohammad Samarrai, a tribal leader from Samarra. He is an ardent horse breeder and discreet gambler who admits going to the races each week. "Here there are owners and gamblers and they are away from politics. This place just feels safe."

"In the month of Ramadan, Baghdad must be seen by night. It has drowsed through the day . . . the sunset gun gives the signal of release. Then it leaps suddenly to life . . ."

—Freya Stark, *Baghdad Sketches*, 1928

family and family occasions, often taking photographs of them.

The City at Night

The night shimmers in Baghdad in normal times—Iraqis renamed it "City of Light" for its magical lights. When reflected in the Tigris, the lights sometimes make it appear to be a river of gold. It is after nine that Baghdad comes alive. In the early years of the sanctions, old traditions died, but they returned in later years. In peaceful times, casual strollers throng the lit squares, laughter rolls through the air, kids play and chase each other. Battered tables and chairs fill side streets, which echo with the clacking of pieces on board games and a million cicada calls ring through the night. Pungent flavors come from dozens of snack sellers—fast food, Arab style—falafel, hummus, and every kind of curried bean.

Sculptures and Monuments

Baghdad has always been a city of artists, and many beautiful and impressive sculptures and monuments dot its streets and squares. Many statues tell the stories

▲ Mohamed Ghani, one of Iraq's most famous sculptors, made many sculptures, such as this one of the flying carpet, which is based on the stories in the book One Thousand and One Nights.

Mohamed Ghani

Mohamed Ghani is one of Iraq's most famous sculptors. Born in Baghdad in 1929, he studied for seven years in Italy and held his first solo exhibition in Baghdad in 1961. In 1962, he became the first professor of sculpture at the Academy of Art in Baghdad. His work can be seen in Rome, Paris, Sicily, and Lebanon as well as in Baghdad where the sculpture (above) of the flying carpet stands. The first Muslim sculptor to be commissioned by the Vatican, he made two huge doors for the largest Catholic church in Baghdad. He was working on them during the 1991 Gulf War when all the electricity was bombed. When it got dark, he took them into the street and everyone in the neighborhood came and held candles for him to work by. "I tell people that we are not just a country of tents and camels. We have a civilization that goes back thousands of years. Culture is in our veins, in our blood."

that revolve around medieval Baghdad, such as Scheherazade and Ali Baba from *One Thousand and One Nights*. Others celebrate the Iraq's ancient past, as in the statue of Hammurabi, the great Babylonian king and lawmaker who lived from 1792 to 1750 B.C. At the airport stands the statue of Abbas bin Firnas, the philosopher and poet, who, in the ninth century, was so certain of the possibility of human flight that he fashioned wings from feathers and tried to fly.

Others refer to more recent events. The statue on Sa'adoun Street commemorates Prime Minister Abdul Muhsin al Sa'adoun, who killed himself inside the Parliament building in 1929 rather than give in to the British. An extraordinary monument from the Iran-Iraq war honors a pilot who flew into an Iranian plane that was about to bomb Baghdad and averted disaster. His statue stands in front of the former Air Force Ministry, surrounded by the remains of his plane. The most famous monument, the Tomb of the Unknown Soldier, was built in 1982 in tribute to the soldiers who died in the Iran-Iraq war. What looks like a flying saucer in fact represents a traditional Iraqi shield, dropped from a dying soldier's hand. Perhaps the most impressive monument is the huge turquoise dome of the Martyrs' Monument, a memorial to the half million Iraqis who died in the Iran-Iraq war. In a huge underground hall, the names of all those who died are inscribed in gold on black marble. The dome is divided into two halves to allow the souls of the dead to fly to heaven.

The Arts and Museums

There are many famous Baghdadi artists, sculptors, and writers, although war has taken its toll on them. A skilled painter and director of the Iraqi National Art Museum, Laila al Attar organized many international

▼ *Sandbags did not prevent the Iraq National Museum in Baghdad, below, from being looted during the 2003 war and stripped of much of its priceless collection dating back to the dawn of civilization. Some items have now been recovered.*

exhibitions and promoted women's art in Iraq. She was killed in a U.S. bombing raid in 1993, two years after the Gulf War ended. An alleged plot to assassinate former president George H.W. Bush prompted the raid. Artists such as Jewad Selim, Mohamed al Hassani, Miran al Sa'di, Ismail Fattah, and Mohamed Ghani have worked in Baghdad.

There are many museums in the city, housing some of the world's earliest treasures. Although they were spared during the bombing, Iraqis and soldiers from many nations looted many of these, however, during the 2003 war. The Iraq Museum in Museum Square contained many archaeological treasures, while the Baghdad Museum, on Mamoun Street, held sculptures of traditional professions and displays about popular customs. The War Museum displayed collections of old weapons and models of imaginatively reconstructed bombed buildings. The National Museum of Modern Art on Kifah Street contained a fantastic collection of Iraqi and foreign modern art. Iraqi experts have been able to restore some of the buildings and artifacts for display, but as of early 2005, museums were currently open only on special occasions.

Movies and Theater

During Saddam Hussein's rule, there was no room for controversial plays, but comedy was highly popular. With its revolving stage, the one thousand-seat National Theater was one of the most modern and well equipped in the Arab world but was looted during the 2003 war. The theaters in Baghdad's central Thawra Street and the cinemas in Sa'adoun Street were busy, especially over the Muslim weekend. Popular Egyptian comedians performed to packed theaters. Despite the sanctions, there was a blossoming film industry too, although movies had to be short because film was so expensive.

Since Saddam Hussein fell, theaters have managed to mount a few successful productions. One Baghdad theater was able to get nearly eight hundred people a night to come see a production during the holiday marking the end of Ramadan. As soon as the holiday ended, however, the number in the audience dropped to eighteen.

Music

Iraqis have a passion for music. Every year since 1987, musicians from up to sixty countries came to stay in Baghdad in August and traveled to ancient Babylon daily to play their music from early morning until late into the night at the famed Babylon Festival. The oldest traditional instrument is the *oud*, believed to have been invented in 1500 B.C. It looks like a beautiful, rounded banjo, inlaid in exotic woods in designs depicting flowers, animals, or whatever takes the artisan's fancy.

During the years of sanctions, Baghdad's world famous National Symphony Orchestra could not even get spare parts for their flutes, lutes, oboes, and violins. In December 2003, the orchestra and its conductor played in Washington at the invitation of President George W. Bush.

CHAPTER 6

Looking Forward

What can anyone say about the future of Baghdad? As of 2005, insurgent activities and battles with U.S.-led security forces still threaten daily life. Most people who live there now want peace, want to be able to live their lives, to go to work and school, to relax in the park, do their shopping, and go to school without worrying about being bombed or killed.

It will not be easy. A 2003 United Nations and World Bank report estimated that it would cost $55 billion to rebuild Iraq's transportation network, hospitals, schools, sewage and electricity plants, and other structures destroyed by bombs over the years. Other estimates put the cost at $100 billion. In 2004, international donors pledged $36 billion toward this rebuilding effort. One UN document estimated that it would cost $92 million to restore the infrastructure, water, and sanitation in Baghdad alone. It is hard to invest this money in Baghdad or Iraq, however, when the situation remains so unsafe.

It is difficult to know how many Iraqis have died since the invasion in 2003; the U.S. Army does not provide body counts. As

◀ *Iraqi children are pictured here enjoying a ride on a large swing on first day of Eid al Adha, or the three-day Feast of the Sacrifice, in central Baghdad. During this celebration, Muslims visit loved ones who have died, cleaning their graves and praying for their souls.*

"I see the countless unremembered acts of kindness and of love that fill their desolate days . . . This region has always led to somewhere worth going. Baghdad is just as glorious in its ruin as it was in its glory, for something noble crawls from the rubble . . ."

—William Paul Roberts, author and journalist, in the *Globe and Mail*, 2003.

of January 2005, lower estimates range from fifteen thousand civilians; upper estimates reach one hundred thousand. No one knows what percentage of these people lived in Baghdad, but there are probably more than six thousand dead Baghdadis. Many are women and children. Many children die when they accidentally come into contact with unexploded ammunition, bombs, and land mines. Also, many Iraqis are ill or even dying from pollution left by the bombings.

Two Views of the Future

In the pessimistic view, as long as foreign troops are in Iraq, bloodshed will continue. Iraqis are being killed, their homes raided, and many are taken to prisons by troops without being accused of anything. There are seventeen thousand prisoners, mostly under U.S. control, and there has been much publicity about torture that has been perpetrated by U.S. and British soldiers. Roadside bombs, mortar assaults, shootings, and insurgent suicide attacks are all part of daily life. Every time someone is killed or arrested, it is possible that more Iraqis may get angry and join the insurgency.

Many of Iraq's educated classes have been killed and many students are afraid to go to school. Four million Iraqis are still in exile and thousands have fled the country. There is a danger that only the poor and uneducated will be left, and Iraq's future will be one of poverty and illiteracy.

There is also a danger that the country will end up divided in three—the south, including Basra, the north, including Mosul, and the Kurdish area in the north—with the country's oil deposits hotly disputed among them. Foreign, not Iraqi, companies would probably run these fields, however.

In 2005, it was difficult to form a government because there were many things people could not agree on. Some complain that too few Sunnis are included. In addition, the government is likely to be $4.4 billion short of what it needs to run the country.

More optimistically, the people of Baghdad, whether Sunni, Shiite, or Christian, Arab or Kurdish, have lived together and socialized over generations. Despite all the invasions and destruction, Iraqis have rebuilt together, shared, and triumphed over hardship and grief. They have retained their ancient culture, welcoming anyone who shares and respects their love of that culture. Baghdadis and all Iraqis are a proud people who do not give up easily. They believe that their city will rise again from the ashes.

Time Line

c. 6500 b.c. People begin farming in Mesopotamia, the land that is now Iraq.

c. 3500 b.c. Civilization of Sumer arises in the region of present-day Iraq.

2049–538 b.c. Babylonians rule the area of present-day Iraq.

539 b.c. Persians begin rule of area.

a.d. 637 Arabs conquer the Persians in present-day Iraq, bringing the religion of Islam.

762 Caliph Abu Ja'afur al Mansur founds the round city of Baghdad.

1055 Tughril Beg conquers Iraq and founds a dynasty.

1096-1291 Christian Crusaders come from Europe to conquer the Holy Land. Saladin, an Iraqi Kurd, fights and defeats the Crusaders.

1258 Hülegü Khan, leader of the Mongols, invades and reduces Baghdad to rubble.

1401 Tamerlane sacks Baghdad and kills its residents.

1534 Süleyman the Magnificent from Turkey overthrows the Mongols and starts the Ottoman rule of Baghdad and Iraq.

1860s Midhat Pasha becomes governor of Baghdad and makes many improvements.

1917 The British take Baghdad and defeat the Ottomans.

1918 Ottoman Empire collapses; France takes over northern Iraq while Great Britain controls southern Iraq.

1921 British crown King Faisal I as puppet king.

1932 Iraq becomes independent of Great Britain.

1943 The Ba'ath Party is formed to promote the idea of a wider Arab nation made of all the Arab states.

1958 Iraqi army executes Faisal II and declares Iraq a republic under Brigadier General Abdul Karim el-Kassem's leadership.

1979 Saddam Hussein becomes president of Iraq, killing thousands of opponents.

1980 Iraq goes to war with its neighbor Iran. By the end of the war in 1988, over one million Iranians and Iraqis have died.

1990 Iraq invades Kuwait. The UN launches the Gulf War, in January 1991, in response.

1990s The UN imposes sanctions on Iraq and a system of nuclear weapons inspections. Approximately 1.5 million children die as a result of the sanctions.

1997 Food and medical supplies from other countries begin to enter Iraq under the United Nations oil-for-food program.

2003 A coalition of troops, mainly from the United States and Great Britain, invade Iraq to oust Saddam Hussein. Bombs destroy parts of Baghdad. Soldiers capture Saddam.

2005 Democratic elections are held in Iraq in January to elect members of the National Assembly. The assembly chooses a president and approves his choice of a prime minister.

Glossary

alchemy a chemical philosophy from the Middle Ages that vainly tried to turn base metals into gold.

caliph the main religious and civil leader of a Muslim community.

cease-fire an agreement between both sides to stop fighting for a certain period of time.

civil servants people employed by the government to run different services. People must pass exams to enter the civil service.

coup the overthrow of a government by a small, usually armed, group.

denominations large groups of religious organizations united under a common faith.

dynasty a family that rules a country for several generations.

exports goods sold by a country to others.

imports goods bought and brought into a country.

infrastructure the system of public works, such as water, roads, and electricity, in a region.

insurgents people who use weapons to revolt against the government.

liberation the act of freeing people from oppression or foreign control.

martyr one who dies for a cause or for his or her homeland.

metropolis a large city.

minaret a slender tower of a mosque with one or more balconies from which the Islamic faithful are called to prayer.

occupation invasion, conquest, and control of an area by foreign armies.

resistance fighters members of an underground organization that are fighting for their country's liberation from a military occupation.

sanctions the blocking of trade to a certain country in hopes of cutting that country off from the world in order to achieve a political objective.

secular not religious.

Shiite Muslims Muslims who believe that religious authority must lie with a direct descendant of the Prophet Muhammad.

Sunni Muslims Muslims who believe that religious authority must lie with the person chosen by the community as the Muslim most qualified to be leader.

subsidized assisted by money given by a government to a person or group for a common good.

terrorist a person or group of people who unlawfully use or threaten violence to achieve what they want, often killing innocent people in the process. One person's terrorists, however, may sometimes be seen by another as freedom fighters who are prepared to use force to free their country or people.

World Bank an international organization that provides loans, advice, and technical assistance to low- and middle-income countries to reduce poverty.

Further Information

Books

Arnold, Catherine. *Baghdad: The Bradt Mini Guide.* Bradt Travel Guides, 2004.

Fast, April. *Iraq: The Culture.* Lands, Peoples, and Cultures (series). Crabtree Publishing Company, 2004.

Heide, Florence Parry, and Judith Heide Gilliland. *House of Wisdom.* DK Ink, 1999.

Martin, Michael. *The Iraqi Prisoner Abuse Scandal.* Lucent Terrorism Library (series). Lucent Books, 2005.

Parks, Peggy J. *Iraq.* Nations in Crisis (series). Blackbirch Press, 2005.

Richie, Jason. *Iraq and the Fall of Saddam Hussein.* Oliver Press, 2003.

Wingate, Brian. *Saddam Hussein* Biographies of Arab World Leaders. (series). Rosen Publishing Group, 2004.

Web Sites

www.arab.net/iraq/iq_media.htm
This Web site from Saudi Arabia gives information on Iraq's history, geography, businesses, and the state of its media under Saddam Hussein.

www.cia.gov/cia/publications/factbook/geos/iz.html
Explore this U.S. government Web site to find facts and statistics on Iraq's economy, military, transnational issues, geography, people, government, and transportation.

www.nationalgeographic.com/index.html
Use the search word Iraq *on this National Geographic magazine home page to find a profile of Iraq plus many other articles, maps, and photos.*

www.pbs.org/wgbh/pages/frontline/shows/saddam
This Public Broadcasting System site explores how Saddam Hussein ruled for so long and the history of the Kurds in Iraq.

www.socialstudiesforkids.com/subjects/iraq.htm
Find Web links about the country and people of Iraq going back to Mesopotamia.

www.timeforkids.com/TFK/news/story/0,6260,362263,00.html
Follow a time line for Iraq and read about Iraq from the ancient civilization of Sumer in Mesopotamia to the current conflict between Iraq and the allied countries of the United States and Great Britain.

www.worldalmanacforkids.com/explore/nations/iraq.html
Learn more about Iraq's population, climate, government, complicated history, and principal cities with this World Almanac Web site.

Index

Page numbers in **bold** indicate pictures.